JONGLEUR
JUGGLER
CARTOONS

Karl-Heinz Ziethen

Der Berliner Karl-Heinz Ziethen gilt als international geschätzter Jongleurexperte. Wie kaum ein anderer beschäftigt er sich seit dreißig Jahren mit dem Fachgebiet, hat in dieser Zeit eine umfangreiche Spezialsammlung aufgebaut und verfügt über Kontakte zu den bedeutendsten Jongleuren der Gegenwart.

1982 erschien von ihm in Paris ein zweibändiges Bildwerk "4000 Years of Juggling", 1984 in Berlin "Jonglierkunst im Wandel der Zeit", 1985 "Juggling – The Art and its Artists" und 1986 "Die Kunst der Jonglerie" (DDR).

Für die Herausgabe dieses Buches hat der Autor Karl-Heinz Ziethen 79 der besten Jongleurkarikaturen aus seiner Sammlung ausgewählt, einige von ihnen wurden sogar von den Jongleuren selbst gezeichnet. Wir hoffen, die Leser können über die Welt der Jongleure ebenso lachen wie wir.

Verlag Rausch & Lüft

arl-Heinz Ziethen, from Berlin, is known internationally as an expert
n juggling. For thirty years he has busied himself with the subject like
o one else. In this time he has built an extensive collection of photos,
ooks and other items pertaining to juggling. More than just a collector,
e is considered a close friend to the most important jugglers of our
ne.

1982, his two-volume photo-book "4000 Years of Juggling" was pub-
hed in Paris. In 1984 "Juggling Through the Ages (German text), in 1985
uggling – The Art and its Artists" and in 1988 in the GDR "The Art of
uggling" (German text) were published in Berlin.

or this book, the author has chosen 79 of the best juggling-cartoons from
s collection. Some of them even are drawn by the jugglers themselves.
e hope the reader will find the world of juggling as humourous as
e have.

Rausch & Lüft, Publishers

LIN 1988

Der Jongleur ist Herr
über die Schwerkraft
Der Karikaturist ist Herr
über den Dargestellten

The juggler is a master
of gravity
The cartoonist is a master
of the person he portrays

Karl-Heinz Ziethen

„Ah… wo hab' ich jetzt die vierte Keule hingeworfen?… Na ja, willkommen zur „Jonglier-Karikaturenschau."

"Ah… where did I throw the fourth club?… Well, welcome to the "juggling-cartoon show."

5

Man glaubt hier gern, daß der Artist
ein „Meister der Balance" ist.

Er balanciert auf einem Bein,
auf Händen kann er's auch sehr fein,

kurz, was er zeigt, ist ganz famos
und der Applaus entsprechend groß.

Doch bringt zum Schluß ein kleiner Ball
den Meister und den Ruf zu Fall.

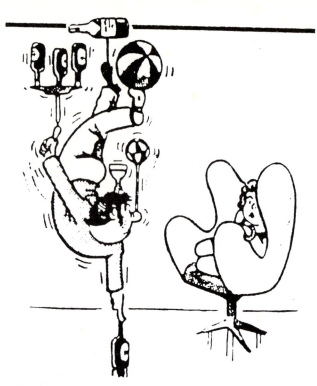

„Du vergeudest nur deine Zeit,
Fred – ich liebe nun mal Peter ...!"

"You waste your time, Fred – I am in love with Peter...!"

,Ia. der tut's nicht anders, er war nämlich früher "Jongleur!"

"Yeah, he always does it like that, he used to be a juggler."

(Zeichnung: Lutugin)

„Was, Otto? Noch 14 Tage, und wir können zum Varieté gehen!"

"Hey, Otto! In 14 days we will be ready for the stage!"

Key

Der kranke Jongleur. — „Heute fühlt er sich schon bedeutend besser, Herr Doktor!"

The sick juggler. – "He's feeling much better today, doctor."

„Ich wollte sie eigentlich um ihre Hand bitten, aber jetzt zögere
ich doch!"

"I actually wanted to ask her for her hand, but now I hesitate!"

"He can't even ride a bicycle!"

„Die phantastischste Nummer, die seit langem hier war. — Mensch, sieh bloß, er jongliert sich selbst mit!"

"The best act they've had here in a long time. – Man, he's even juggling himself!"

„Tolle Nummer, haben Sie ein Engagement?"
„Nee, leider, ick jongliere jetzt mit Teppich-
kloppern, Auto-Wischlappen, kaputten Radio-
apparaten und solchen Sachen!"

"Great act, are you performing somewhere?" "No, unfortunately I'm only juggling brooms, wash-rags, broken radios and such things!"

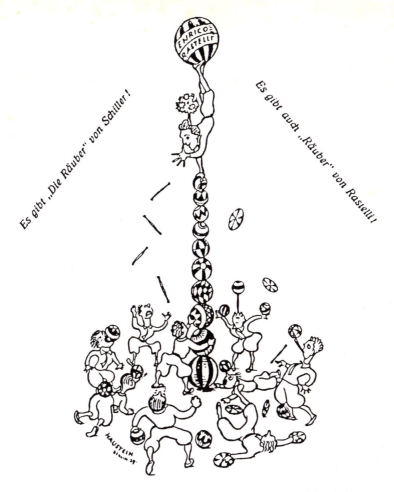

Es gibt „Die Räuber" von Schiller!

Es gibt auch „Räuber" von Rastelli!

There are "The Robbers" from Schiller! There are also "robbers" from Rastelli!

Jenny Jaeger

The artistic director of the Scala to an auditioning performer:
"... And the gold-fishes don't do anything?..."

Der künstlerische Leiter   der Scala
zu einem sich vorstellenden Artisten:
„... Und die Goldfische machen garnichts ?...“

"RECKON HE'S A BIT OF A NOVELTY MABEL"

„Ich glaub' er ist was besonderes, Mabel."

So wird nie etwas aus dir werden, Anthony...

This is not the way you are going to succeed, Anthony...

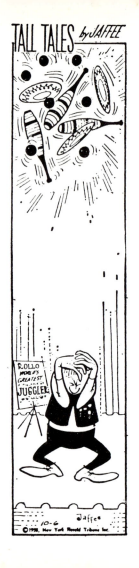

Toly

Michael Moschen

—4—3—2—1—FIRE !!!

... nun, wie ist das passiert!?

"THEY ALWAYS DROP SOMETHING TO
MAKE IT LOOK DIFFICULT"

„Sie lassen immer etwas fallen, damit es schwieriger
aussieht."

„Mein Vater kann das auch"

W. C. FIELDS

MAC TURC & JOE

Jiron
NEW YORK

"THE RIVAL JUGS PASS IN THE STREET"

Zwei Rivalen begegnen sich auf der Straße

Kris Kremo

REINHOLD
DAS
NASHORN

ZIRKUS

Reinhold war mit seinem Neffen
heut im Zirkus anzutreffen.

„So, jetzt schau mal, kleiner Mann,
was dein Onkel alles kann."

„Nur drei Stück? Das ist nicht schwer!
Onkel Reinhold, nimm doch mehr."

„Sieben Tassen, — bitte sehr!"
„Onkel, du bist Chef-Jongleur!"

Seht, wie sicher er es hält.
Das Geschirr wird abgestellt.

„Bravo Onkel, jetzt sind's gleich
siebene auf einen Streich!"

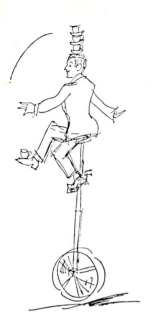

Rudy Horn

at work and…
bei der Arbeit und…

"Another coffee I presume?"

„Noch ein Kaffee vermute ich?"

Kriemhild. is' das ein Ringer?

Kriemhild, isn't he from Ringling?

„Um Himmels willen, Charly, jetzt habe ich vergessen, wie unsere Nummer zu Ende geht!"   „Punch"

"For Christ's sake, Charly, I forgot how our act ends"

Dr. Hot + Neon

Das Duett mit der speziellen Note
The Duet with the special note

I catch five balls

I catch seven balls

I catch five clubs

I catch seven hoops

I catch five larges balls

And now most difficult I
try to catch one husband

Francis Brunn

Der Jongleur, der schneller jongliert als sein Schatten
The juggler who juggles faster than his shadow

Sergei Ignatow

Ein wohl anerkannter russischer Jongleur
A highly respected russian juggler

Frank Eders

Der Mann, der 5 Zentner schwere Granaten mit dem bloßen Nacken auffängt . . . . . .

. . . . zu Hause

46

Toly

Andrew Allen

Teufelsstab
Devil Stick

"THREE SABRES WITH ONE HAND"

„Drei Säbel mit einer Hand"

Kein Engagement… schade, aber mach'
dir nichts daraus, Lane…

… du wirst schon irgendwo
reinrutschen.

Napoleon mit seinem äußerst interessanten Dreiball-Trick

Napoleon with his most interesting Three Ball Trick

Im Bett ist er auch einmalig!

Fidel Castro's revolutionäre Idee zur Verwendung leerer Zigarrenkisten

Fidel Castro's revolutionary idea for the use of empty cigar boxes

„Jonglieren ist sehr gut für die Konzentration –
aber Konzentration kann auch sehr gut für das Jonglieren sein"

"Assuming the toilet roll is the Earth and the coffee grinder the moon, then the teddy bear is ...er." Mr. Watson tried for the umpteenth time to explain the universe to his son .....

Angenommen die Klopapierrolle ist die Erde und die Kaffeemaschine der Mond, dann ist der Teddy… äh…!"
Herr Becker versuchte zum wiederholten Male, seinem Sohn das Weltall zu erklären…

Einstein, während er relativ leicht entdeckt, daß die unvermeidliche Anziehungskraft eines sich bewegenden Objektes der... Boden ist.

Einstein discovering relatively easy the inevitable attraction of an object in motion is the... floor.

"I TOLD YOU NOT TO STAND TOO CLOSE ELMER!"

„Ich habe dir doch gesagt, daß du nicht zu nahe herangehen sollst, Elmer!"

He is a genius. He reduced juggling into it's archaic original form!

Karikaturen Register
Cartoon Index

Deutsche Zeitungskarikatur, 1942
German newspaper cartoon, 1942

Deutsche Zeitungskarikatur, 1958
German newspaper cartoon, 1958

Enrico Rastelli (I) „Das Non Plus Ultra" der Jongleure, Werbeanzeige.
Karikatur Haustein, Berlin 1929
Enrico Rastelli (I) The "Non Plus Ultra" of jugglers, advertisement.
Cartoon Haustein, Berlin 1929

Jenny Jaeger, (Deutsch-Russin). Jonglierte 1924 erstmalig mit 9 + 10 Bällen. Karikatur, Toly 1987
Jenny Jaeger (Russian-German). Juggled 9 + 10 balls for the first time in 1924. Cartoon, Toly 1987

Karikatur Scala Varietéprogrammheft, Berlin 1936
Cartoon Scala Varietémagazine, Berlin 1936

Karikatur von Joe Marsh (GB), 1950
Cartoon from Joe Marsh (GBR), 1950

Anthony Gatto (USA). Jugendliches Jongleurwunder. Karikatur Toly, 1983
Anthony Gatto (USA). Youthful juggling wonder. Cartoon Toly, 1983

Amerikanische Zeitungskarikatur von Jaffee, 1958
American newspaper cartoon from Jaffee, 1958

Michael Moschen (USA). Karikatur Toly, 1987
Michael Moschen (USA). Cartoon Toly, 1987

„Im Club" (englisches Wort club = Keule). Karikatur Toly, 1985
"Club" Cartoon Toly, 1985

Wallastons (D). Karikatur Mac Morland, Berlin 1931 – Deutsche Zeitungskarikatur, 1980
Wallastons (G). Cartoon Mac Morland, Berlin 1931 – German newspaper cartoon, 1980

Karikatur von Joe Marsh (GB), 1950
Cartoon from Joe Marsh (GBR), 1950

Karikatur von Philip J. Berube (USA), 1980
Cartoon from Philip J. Berube (USA), 1980

Karikatur von Joe Marsh (GB), 1951
Cartoon from Joe Marsh (GBR), 1951

31 Karikatur von Philip J. Berube (USA), 1960
Cartoon from Philip J. Berube (USA), 1960

32 W. C. Fields (USA). Bekannt auch als Filmkomiker. Karikatur W. C. Fields, 1909
W. C. Fields (USA). Also famous as film comedian. Cartoon W. C. Fields, 1909

33 Mac Turc (A). Karikatur Whiron, 1936
Mac Turc (AUT). Cartoon Whiron, 1936

34 Karikatur von Joe Marsh (GB), 1951
Cartoon from Joe Marsh (GBR), 1951

35 Deutsche Zeitungskarikatur, 1955
German newspaper cartoon, 1955

36 Kris Kremo (CH). Weltmeister im Pirouettendrehen mit Zigarrenkisten. Karikatur Peter Pelanda,
rich 1975 – Karikatur von Philip J. Berube (USA), 1979
Kris Kremo (CH). Worldmaster in pirouettes with cigar boxes. Cartoon Peter Pelanda, Zürich 197
Cartoon from Philip J. Berube (USA), 1979

37 Amerikanische Zeitungskarikatur, 1957
American newspaper cartoon, 1957

38 „Reinhold das Nashorn." Karikatur Loriot (D), 1954
"Reinhold the Rhino." Cartoon Loriot (FRG), 1954

39 Rudy Horn (D). Sein Markenzeichen, das Werfen und Fangen von Tellern und Tassen vom Fuß
den Kopf. Zeitungskarikatur, Oslo 1967 – Karikatur Toly, 1970
Rudy Horn (G). His trademark was kicking saucers and cups from his foot on to the top of his he
Newspaper cartoon, Oslo 1967 – Cartoon Toly, 1970

40 Bob Bramson (D). Zeitungskarikatur zur Friedrichstadt Palastprogrammbesprechung, Berlin 195
Bob Bramson (FRG). Newspaper cartoon of Friedrichstadt Palast program review, Berlin 1957

41 Deutsche Zeitungskarikatur (Punch), 1938
German newspaper cartoon (Punch), 1938

42 Dr. Hot + Neon (USA/Kanada). Jonglierend mit 6 Banjos während sie das „An die Freude"-Thema
Beethovens 9. Symphonie spielen. Karikatur Toly, 1987
Dr. Hot + Neon (USA/Canada). Juggling with 6 banjos while playing the "An die Freude"-theme fr
Beethovens Ninth Symphony. Cartoon Toly, 1987

43 Trixie (A). Meisterjongleuse. Ihr schwierigster Trick, einen Ehemann zu fangen! Karikatur Toly, 198
Trixie (AUT). Cartoon Toly, 1987

Francis Brunn (D). Jongleurlegende zu Lebzeiten. Karikatur Toly, 1987
Francis Brunn (FRG). A juggling legend in his own life time. Cartoon Toly, 1987

Sergei Ignatow (SU). Berühmtester Jongleur der UdSSR; jonglierte 1973 erstmalig mit 11 Reifen. Karikatur Toly, 1982
Sergei Ignatow (URS). Famousest juggler of soviet union; juggled 11 rings for the first time in 1973. Cartoon Toly, 1982

Frank Eders (A). Humoristischer Kraft-Jongleur. Karikatur Scala Varietéprogrammheft, Berlin 1939
Frank Eders (AUT). Humorous Strong-Man juggler; the man who catches a 500 pound shell on his neck. Cartoon Scala Varieté magazine, Berlin 1939

Andrew Allen (USA). Chinesisches Stockspiel, genannt das „Spiel mit dem Teufelsstab." Karikatur Toly, 1985
Andrew Allen (USA). "Devil Stick" Cartoon Toly, 1985

Karikatur von Michel Lauziere, Quebec 1980
Cartoon from Michel Lauziere, Quebec 1980

Deutsche Zeitungskarikatur von Nabil El-Solami, DDR 1982
German newspaper cartoon from Nabil El-Solami, GDR 1982

Amerikanische Zeitungskarikatur, 1965
American newspaper cartoon, 1965

Deutsche Zeitungskarikatur von Willy Moese, DDR 1982
German newspaper cartoon from Willy Moese, GDR 1982

„Napoleon" Karikatur Toly, 1987
"Napoleon" Cartoon Toly, 1987

Amerikanische Zeitungskarikatur, 1966
American newspaper cartoon, 1966

„Fidel Castro" Karikatur Toly, 1987
"Fidel Castro" Cartoon Toly, 1987

Russische Zeitungskarikatur von A. Gawrileow, 1979
Russian newspaper cartoon from A. Gawrileow, 1979

Russische Zeitungskarikatur von K. Moschlein, 1979
Russian newspaper cartoon from K. Moschlein, 1979

Englische Zeitungskarikatur, 1984
British newspaper cartoon, 1984

58 „Seifenblasen" Karikatur Paul Degen (CH), 1987
   "Soap-Bubbles" Cartoon Paul Degen (CH), 1987

59 Deutsche Zeitungskarikatur von Papan, Stern-Magazin 1985
   German newspaper cartoon from Papan, Stern magazine 1985

60 „Mondjongleur" Karikatur Peter Davidson, USA 1985
   "Moon juggler" Cartoon Peter Davidson, USA 1985

61 „Einstein" Karikatur Toly, 1987
   "Einstein" Cartoon Toly, 1987

62 Karikatur von Joe Marsh (GB), 1952
   Cartoon from Joe Marsh (GBR), 1952

63 Deutsche Zeitungskarikatur von Kazu, 1983
   German newspaper cartoon from Kazu, 1983

64 „Straßen-Jongleur" Karikatur Toly, 1988
   "Street juggler" Cartoon Toly, 1988

65 „Charlie Chaplin" Karikatur Toly, 1985
   "Charlie Chaplin" Cartoon Toly, 1985

Titelinnenseite (front inside): King Repp (1932), Béla Kremo (1957), Rebla (1935), Paul Cinquevalli (19
Ernest Montego (1958), Felix Adanos (1930)

Buchrückeninnenseite (back cover inside): Salerno (1925), Bobby May (1934), Massimiliano Truzzi (193
G. W. Woltard (1930), Alexander Kiss (1959), Piletto (1929)
Buchrücken (back cover): Karikatur von Toly, 1988. Cartoon from Toly, 1988

Abbildungsnachweis – Mention of sources

Karikaturen von Joe Marsh (GB, Manchester) Juggler's Bulletin (Tulsa, Oklahoma) 1950-52 (22, 28, 34, 62)
Karikaturen von Philip J. Berube (USA) Juggler's World Magazin (USA) 1979 (29, 36)
Karikatur von Michel Lauziere (Quebec) Juggler's World Magazin (USA) 1980 (48)
Karikatur von A. Gawrileow und K. Moschlein (SU) Zirkus + Estrade Magazin, Moskau 1979 (55, 56)
Karikatur von Loriot (Vico von Bülow), Text von Uecker + Dahl (D). Sternchen Buch, Stuttgart 1954 (3
Karikatur von Papan (D), Stern Magazin, Hamburg 1985 (59)

Besonderen Dank an (many thanks to) Toly – Antole Dedessus le Moutier (Paris) – Chris Adams (Lond
und den kids Andrew + Olli

Verlag Rausch & Lüft

Berlin

ARTISTIK · CIRCUS · VARIETÉ

Karl-Heinz Ziethen & Andrew Allen

JONGLIEREN, Kunst und Künstler

362 Seiten gebunden, 290 Fotos, 8 Farbfotos, 93 Zeichnungen, umfassender Index, Text in dtsch., engl., franz.   ISBN 3-9801140-1-5

Das Buch, mit dem Originaltitel "JUGGLING – The Art and its Artists", ist in englisch verfaßt und hat eine Textbeilage in deutsch und französisch.
Das Buch ist eine umfassende Fotodokumentation der Jonglierkunst von ihren Ursprüngen bis zur Gegenwart. Ein einmaliges Nachschlagewerk, das sowohl Liebhaber als auch Laien begeistern wird.

Karl-Heinz Ziethen

Jonglierkunst im Wandel der Zeiten

36 Seiten geheftet, 68 Abbildungen   Eine Kurzfassung der Jongliergeschichte.

ISBN 3-9801140-0-7

Martin Schaaff

Die Buschens – 100 Jahre Circus Busch

72 Seiten Paperback, 132 Abbildungen

ISBN 3-9801140-3-1

Die lange Freundschaft des Autors mit der Direktorin Paula Busch garantiert die Authenzität der Geschichten über das Auf und Ab eines Berliner Circus, der zu seiner Glanzzeit neben dem Chapiteau vier feste Bauten besaß. Ein nostalgischer und liebevoller Rückblick.

Tillmann Schrader · Lothar Übel u. a.

ARTISTEN – Eine große Familie

48 Seiten Paperback, 63 Abbildungen

ISBN 3-9801140-6-6

Katalog gleichnamiger Ausstellung über die frühere Hochburg der Artistik im Berliner Bezirk Neukölln. Sorgfältig recherchiert, mit einem Interview des "letzten" Gentlemanjongleurs Felix Adanos.

Ken Benge

The Art of Juggling

138 Seiten Paperback, in englisch.

ISBN 3-9801140-4-X

Über 60 Dreiballtricks und mehr werden in diesem Buch ausführlich beschrieben und mit Zeichnungen erläutert.

Artisten- & Circusmotive
– Jongleure –

Serie von 10 Postkarten, in Farbe, Format 10 x 15 cm.

Bestell-Nr.: 9801140-J (1-10)

Enrico Rastelli, W. C. Fields, Joseph Wallenda, 7 Perezoff, Maccette Comp., King Repp, Viktor Viktorow, Bubu, Varieté-Plakat, Circus-Plakat.